Kama Sutra 2

With Bob And Brenda

Dot-To-Dot Edition

Written And Illustrated

By

Paul Gwilliam

Copyright © 2014 Paul J Gwilliam
All Rights Reserved

For Dawn.

You Are My Brenda

Find More Bob And Brenda Books

From Online Book Stores

Disclaimer

Bob and Brenda are not responsible for any injuries you may sustain while attempting anything shown in this book.

A Word About Safe Sex

Practice safe sex and you're less likely to pick up a Sexually Transmitted Infection, HIV or get pregnant.
You must use condoms. Sex and condoms go together like Bob and Brenda. You can't have one without the other.

Remember: More partners means bigger risks. So, have fun but please be careful. For more information please search the web.

Thank you.

Introduction

The book everybody has been waiting for has finally arrived. Kama Sutra 2 with Bob and Brenda has taken over a year to make it to print and now here it is in dot to dot format.

After the success of Kama Sutra with Bob and Brenda, its author and illustrator Paul Gwilliam, decided to give the main characters a face lift and sent them both to the gym.

Now, Bob and Brenda are back looking fabulous and feeling fit enough to make another gruelling Kama Sutra book.

Kama Sutra 2 with Bob and Brenda will have you in stitches while loving it up between the sheets.

More positions than ever before and a few surprises to keep you entertained and feeling sexy.

Go on......You know you want too.

The Positions

10 Past 10

What time is it? It's 10 past 10. Shagging time.

What I really love about this position is how deep it can get and it's a good position for those who love to snog. I sit on the floor and Brenda sits on my lap. I put my Tummy Banana into her Crotch Sink and she lifts and straightens her legs. Wow! That's so deep. I can only last a few seconds in this position.

Look out!!! It's two stroke Bob!

Bob

A Rush Of Blood To The Bed

Have you ever looked at your reflection in the mirror while you're having sex and thought 'That just looks so stupid'?
I caught a glimpse of my reflection in the wardrobe mirror last week, I was doing this position at the time.
Why? I thought. Why put myself through all this just to make sex more interesting? Then it came to me. Sex is boring, so you have to make it interesting and if that means you swing from the lampshade then that's what you must do.
Brenda lies on the bed and I'm standing besides her. I pull her Growler towards me and enter my Cum Gun. She then wraps her legs around my waist. Then it's pump, pump, pump until Brenda's face turns purple. Lol

Bob

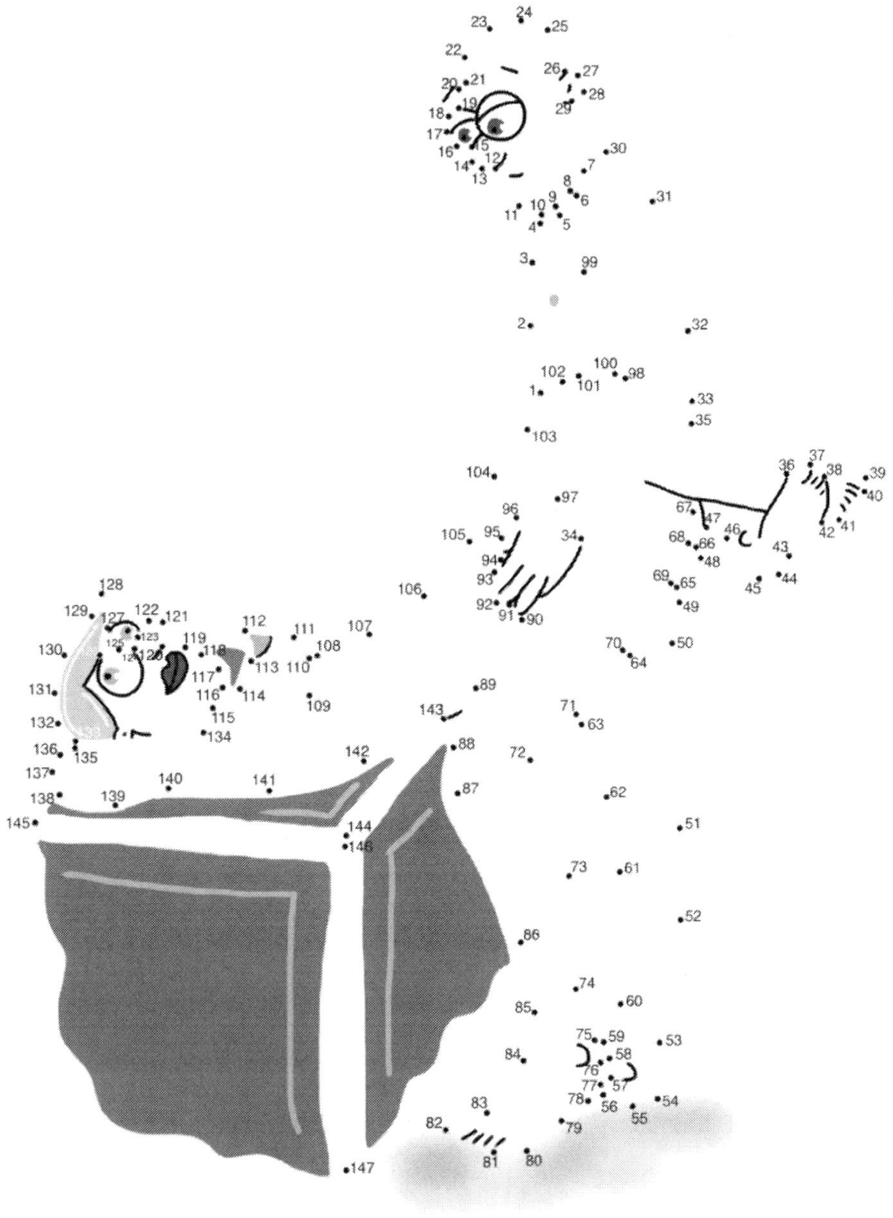

Balance Trick

The magician Paul Daniels used to say "You're gonna like this. Not a lot."
He could have very easily been describing this position because it's a bit of a tricky one to do.
I sit on the edge of the bed and Brenda sits on my Gash Mallet with her back to me. I lean back as she puts her legs behind me. Brenda lifts her body up by pushing up off my knees.

Sounds complicated but the hard part is keeping balanced while I pump Brenda's Flappy Bird. Tweet tweet.

Bob

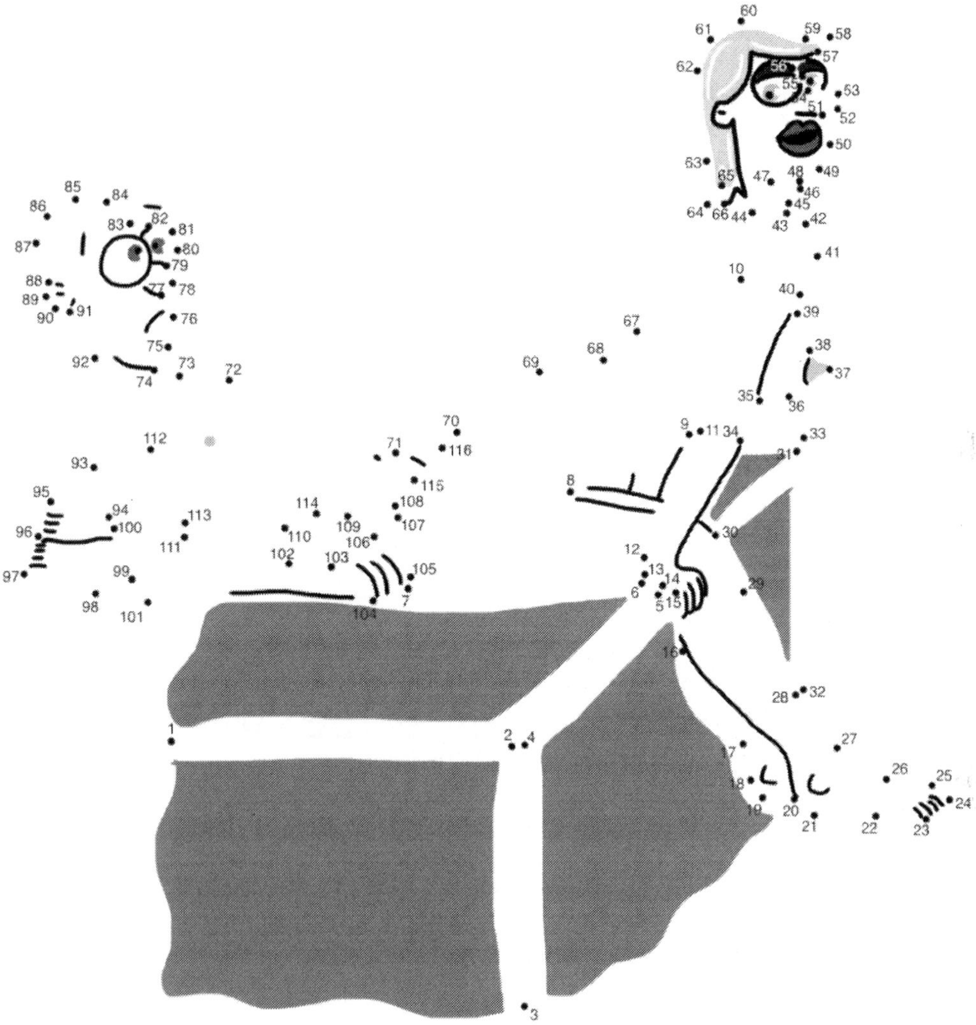

Bum 2 Bum

This is a very weird position but it's strangely a very erotic one too.

This position must be done on the floor because you need plenty of room.
We both lie on the floor in a press up position, heel to heel. Bob slowly reverses his Porridge Gun into my Fur Burger.
You must have a flexible dinger to do this position.
 If you're a young man, forget it!

Brenda

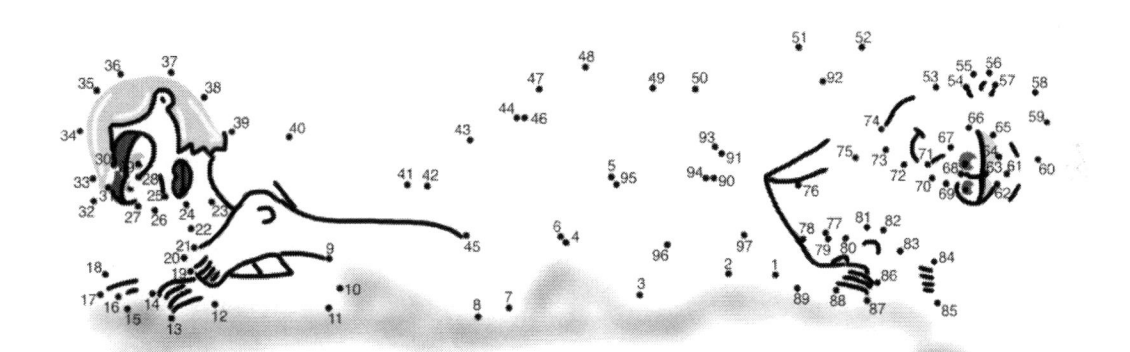

Bum 69

Anything to do with the bum whilst having sex is like marmite. You either love it or hate it. Me and Brenda love it.

We call this the bum 69 because it's basically a 69 where the oral has been replaced with bum licking or rimming. We always set the mood for this by having a good shower, making sure our nether regions are clean and fresh.

Never try this after having a vindaloo.

Bob

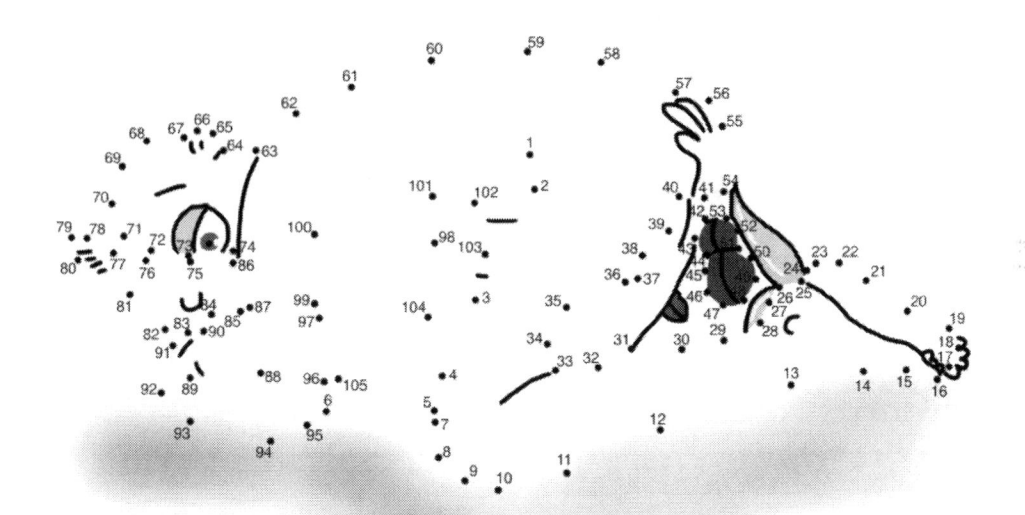

Bum Burn

Grind them buttocks boys!

This is a great position if you like carpet burns on your arse. Lol
It may sound weird but I love the feeling of rough carpet on my plum cheeks.
Bob sits on the floor like a Buddha and I sit between his legs with my feet on his chest.
He puts his Gripper into my Rug and we both start grinding.
Shag pile burns on both our peachy bottoms.

Mmmmmmmmm Ouch!

Brenda

Bum Lick Bend

I love to lick Brenda's brown star. I like nothing more than sticking my tongue right up her chocolate tube. That's why this is another of my favourite positions.

I sit on the floor and Brenda bends down in front of me exposing her Poo Cave. I can easily get my tongue in while Brenda is flexible enough to suck on my Snot Rocket at the same time.
Love it.

Bob

Carry Me Home

Have you ever tried to carry a sack of potatoes whilst trying to get an erection? Trust me it's not easy.

You're best to start this position from a table. The 'Lay the table' position is ideal for this.
Once my Vagina Miner is in Brenda's Cum Dumpster I move away from the table. I then have to hold onto Brenda for dear life. I've lost count of the amount of times I've dropped her. Lol

Bob

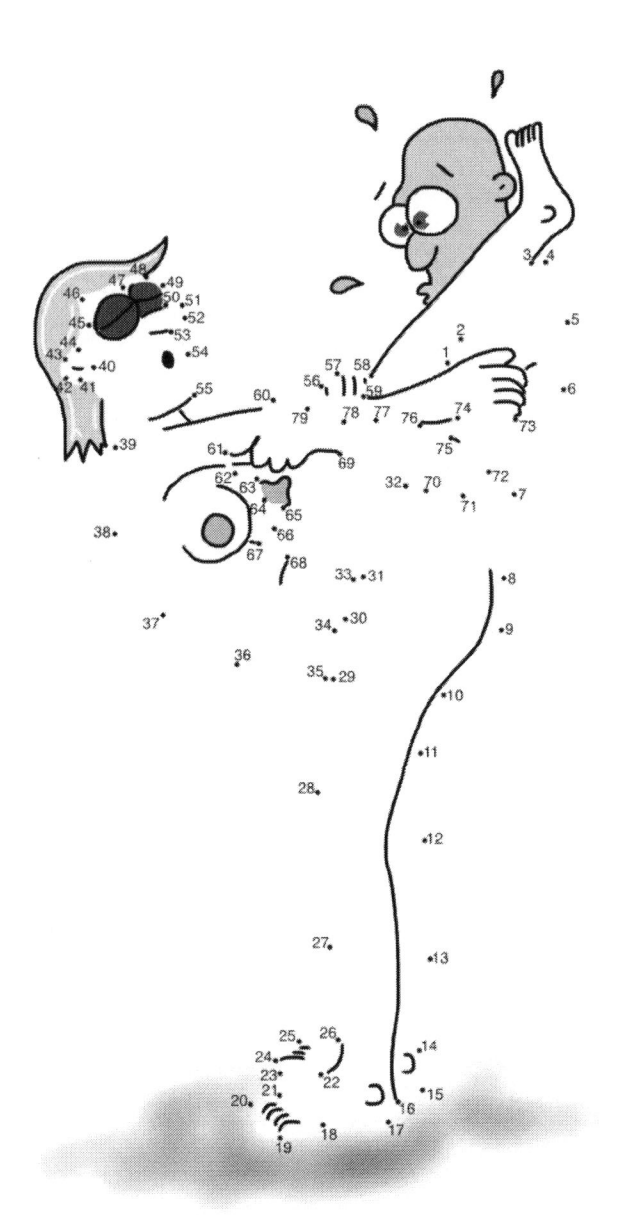

The Centipede

Have you ever seen the film 'The human centipede'?
It's about this sicko man who takes a guy and two women and surgically stitches them together, arse to mouth.
This position is called 'The Centipede' because of that film. There's no surgical procedure involved though.

I go on all fours and Bob is also on all fours behind me. He can lick my Pink Purse and Brown Hole until his tongue is sore. Make sure you're clean before starting this one. You don't want shit up your nose.

Brenda

Chair For Two

Chairs are amazing. You can sit on them, play musical chairs with them, use them to reach high shelves and you can have sex on them.
Don't try this on any old chair though. It needs to be sturdy and strong enough to take both your weight.

Bob sits on the chair and I sit on his lap. Simple. Did I mention his Donger is deep inside my Bald Pie.
Ooooooooh chair you go nicely.

Brenda

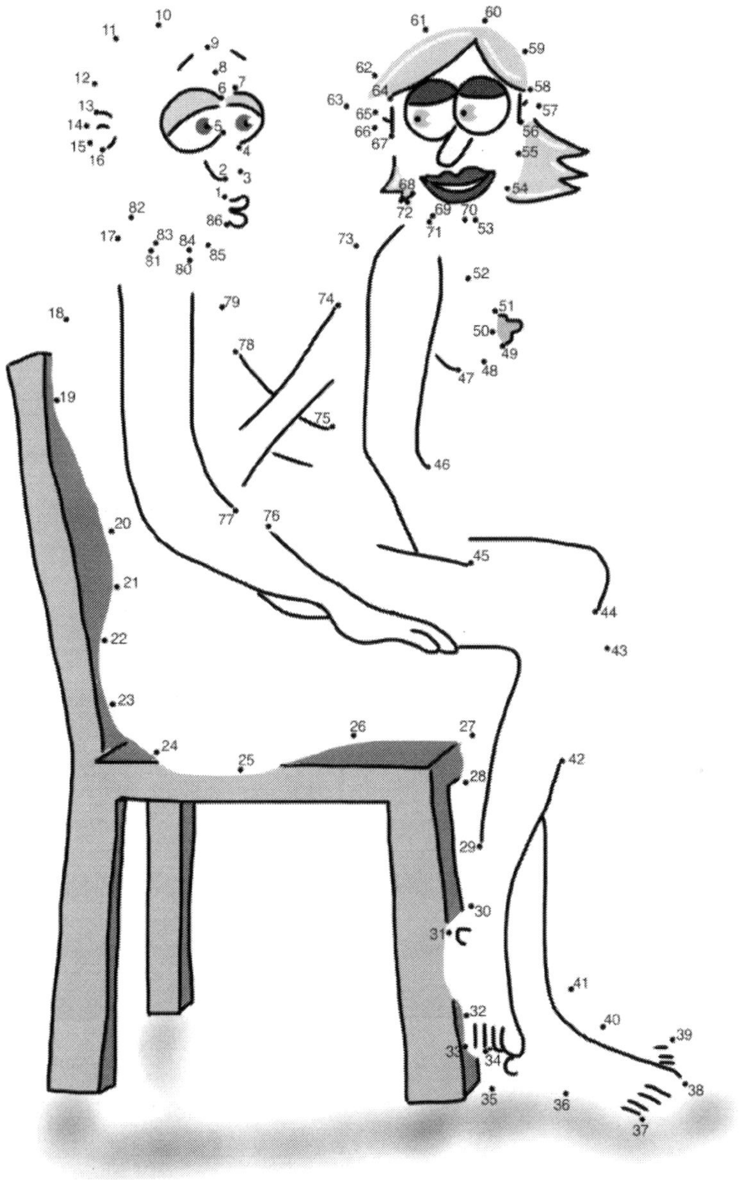

Bob and Brenda like having fun with their best friends, Barry and Betty.
Can you find 8 differences between the 2 pictures below?

(The answers are at the end of the book)

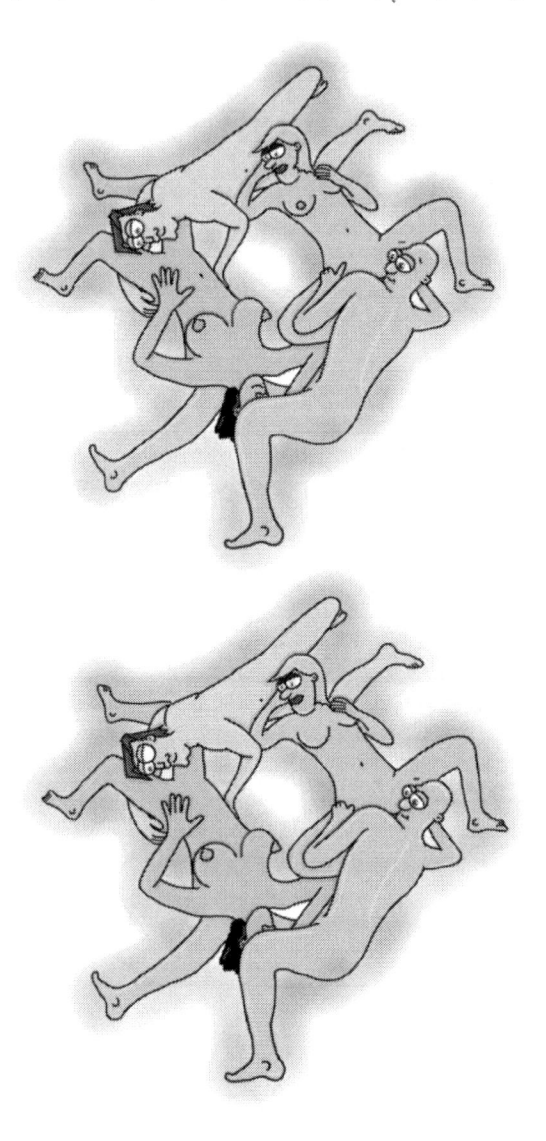

The Choo Choo

I'm just a big kid at heart. When I have some free time I love to play with my train set. I think that's why I enjoy this position so much.

Brenda squats in front of me, then puts her hands on the floor. I kneel behind her and put my Log into her Hot Fire.
CHOO CHOO!!
Ride that love train.

Bob

Cum 'N' Have A Go

This position might look very easy but trust me, it's not.
It kills my arms and Brenda's legs get a good workout too.

I lie back and lift myself up so my body is diagonal to the bed. Brenda then climbs on and I enter my Wobbler into her Lady Gash.

This is a really good workout, especially if I leave all the hard work to Brenda's legs. She looks fantastic thanks to positions like this.

No Pain No Gain.

Bob

Does My Bum Look Big On This?

Any position where I get to stare at Brenda's Butt Hole while my Sausage Torpedo enters her Willy Coffin is alright by me.

I lie on the floor in a sitting up position and Brenda sits on my Love Organ, facing my feet. She leans forward slightly so I can see everything that's going on. Mmmmmm I love it.

By the way Brenda, your bum never looks big on me. It's perfect. X

Bob

The Fall Out

We call this the fall out because it's near impossible to keep my Womb Broom in Brenda's Foetus Factory. Lol

I lie on my back and pull my knees up as high as I can. Brenda then lies on me and I insert my Tiny Tim into her Cratchett. I can then grab hold of her arse to make sure she doesn't slip off my Rocket.

The things I do for a quiet life. Anything for you, Brenda dear.

Bob

Give Me A Leg Up

If there was one position that I would have a bronze statue of Me and Bob made and put on the front lawn, it's this one.
There's something very artistic about it. I think so.
I go on all fours in a doggy position and Bob enters his Knob into my Black Hole. He then lifts either my left or right leg to get a more deeper shafting.

Mmmmmm Cover me in bronze paint and let's go on the front lawn, Bob.

Brenda

The Glider

Just glide it in...........or slide it in.

This is another position which has a deep penetration.

Brenda lies on her back and puts one leg over my shoulder. My Vagina Diver enters her Cum Sponge as I glide my buttocks along her other leg.
Brenda loves this position even though I sometimes leave poo stains on her leg. Lol

Bob

Head Rush

Bob loves to make me look stupid. He says 'I like to see you in an uncomfortable position because it turns me on'.
 WEIRDO.

When I'm lying on my back, Bob lifts my legs up until his Spunk Hose is able to enter my Fish Flapper. It makes me look stupid and uncomfortable.

Bob loves it.

Brenda

The Horsey

This is sure to raise a smile and get you laughing.
It's not the easiest of positions to do but you have to give it a try.

Bob lies on the floor and does what they call 'A crab'. This is where you put your hands behind your head and push yourself up, lifting your back off the floor. Bob can't hold this position for long so I quickly climb on and put his Man Flute into my Coochie Coo.
I slowly ride him until his arms give way and we collapse onto the floor.
I like to tweak his nipples at the same time.
Lol

Brenda

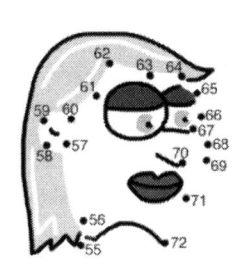

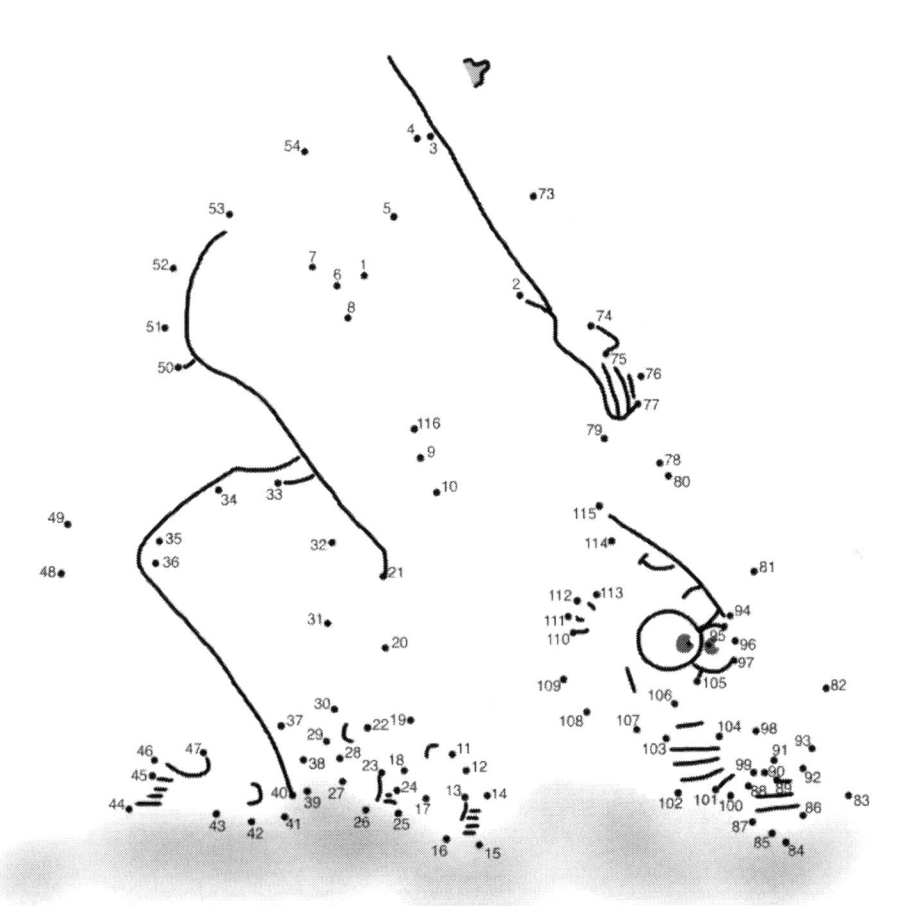

I Spy A Brown Eye

'I spy with my little eye, something beginning with P.H.'

This is a fun one for you to try. Brenda lies on the edge of the bed with her legs in the air.
I bend over and reverse my Fanny Puppet into her Cum Locker.

I get a good view from here.

It was Poo Hole I spied. Lol

Bob

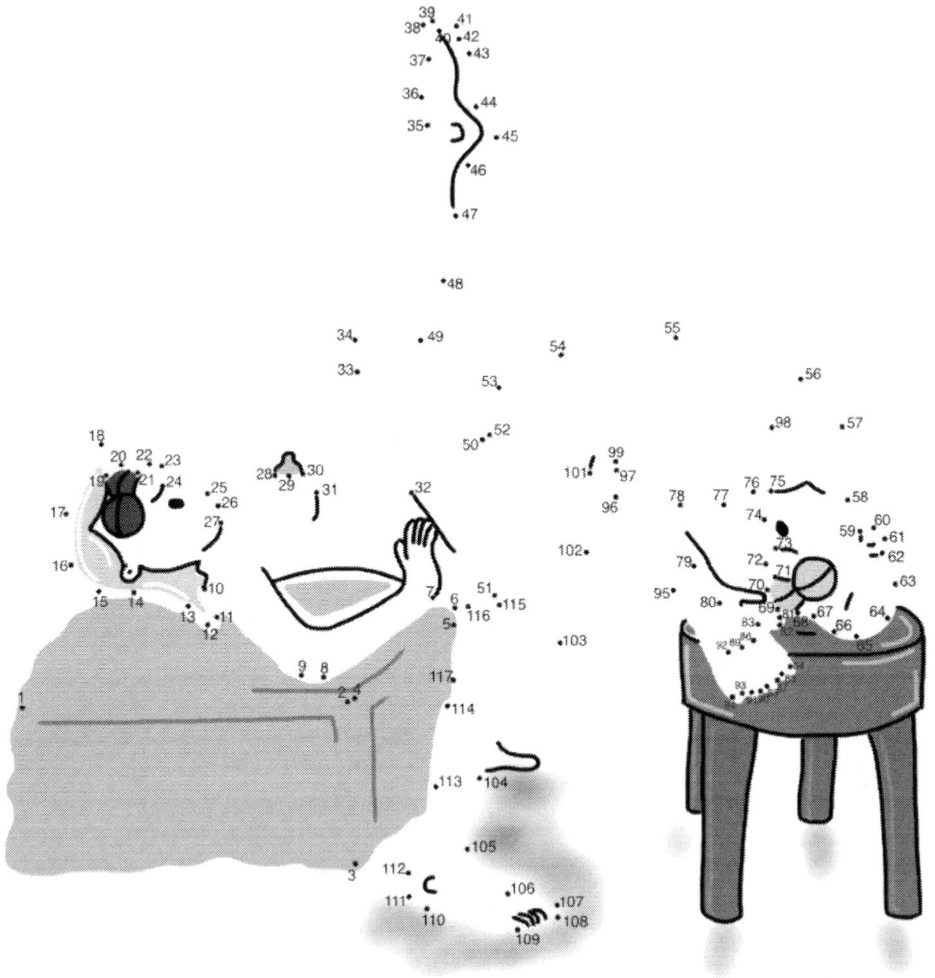

Kiss My Arse

I like to tell Bob to kiss my arse.
He strips me, sits down behind me and
plants a sucker on my Trap Number Two.
I love it when I've showered so he can stab
my butt hole with his tongue.

It's not for everyone.

Brenda

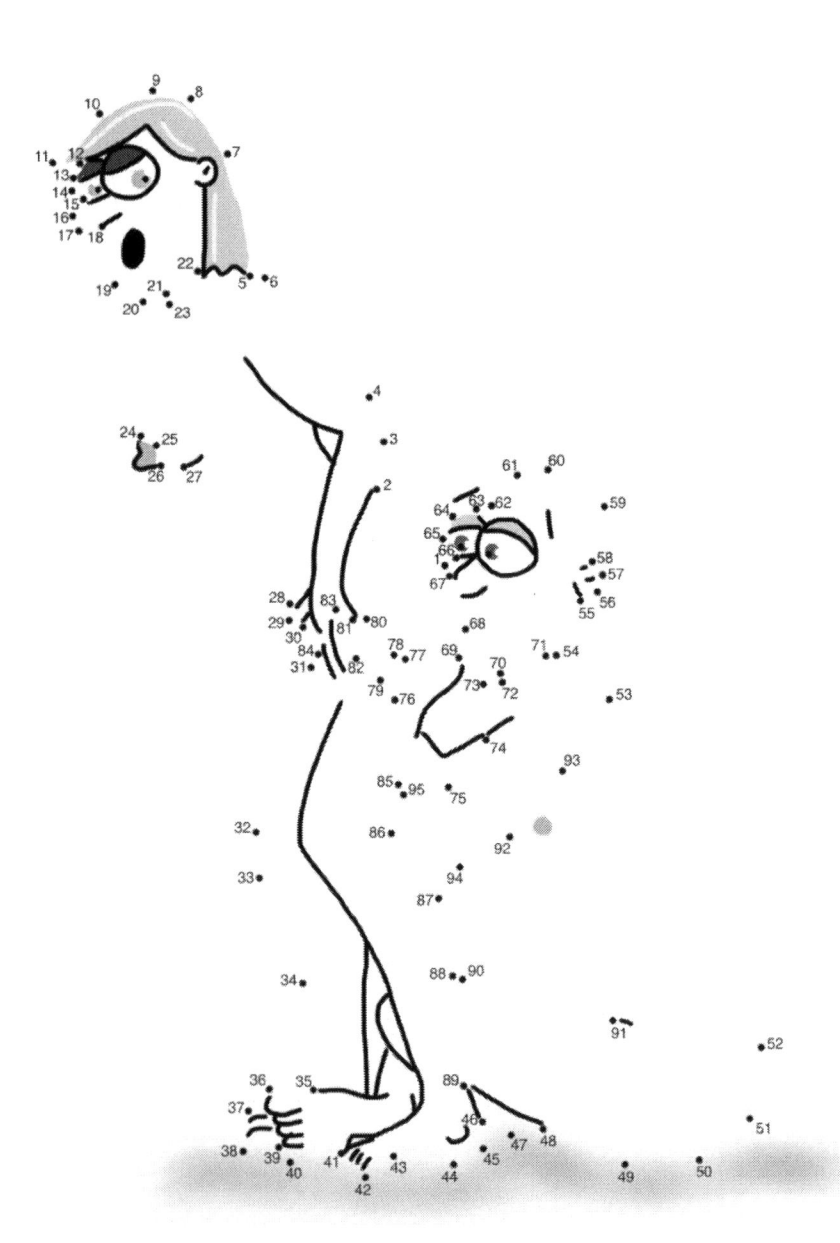

Brenda

Name : Brenda
Age : 44
Hair Colour : Blonde
Eye Colour : Blue
Star sign : Aquarius
Statistics : 36-24-36
Occupation : Bingo caller
Favourite Book : Kama Sutra with Bob and Brenda

Favourite Film : Rocky
Favourite TV Program : Family guy
Favourite Food : Sausage
Hobbies : Shagging, Blow jobs, Anything sexual

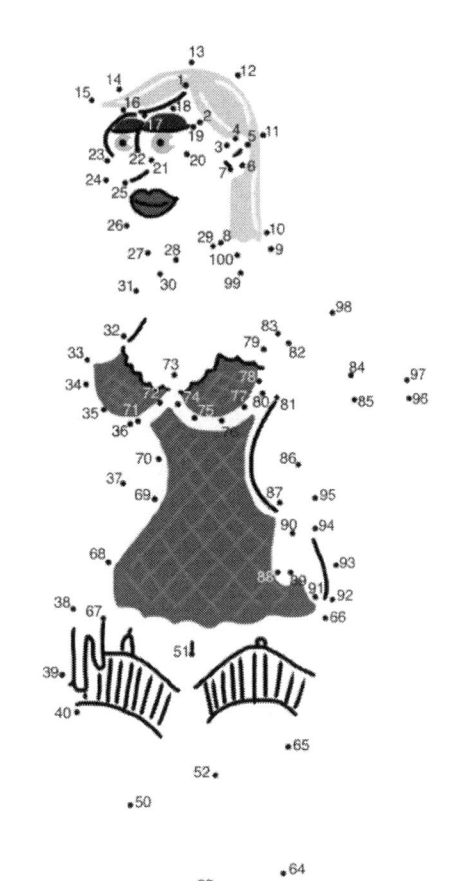

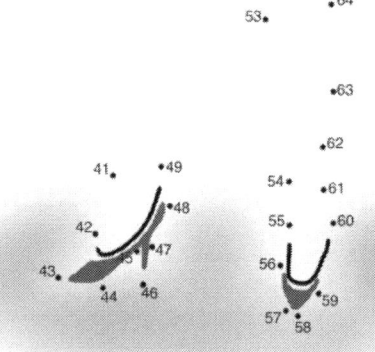

Knees Up Father Bob

If, like me, you grew up in the 70's then you will know what a space hopper is. For those who don't remember, it was a big rubber ball with handles that you sat on and bounced up and down.
They were great!
This position reminds me of a space hopper.

Bob lies on his back and pulls his knees up. I sit on Bob's One-Eyed Monster and bounce up and down until the One-Eyed Monster is sick inside my Jizz Well.

Brenda

The Knee Hugger

I love to watch Brenda's sweaty jugs wobble. Mmmmmm.

Any position that gives me this treat gets a thumbs up from me. The knee Hugger does just that.

I sit on the floor and Brenda lies down in front of me. She slowly moves towards me until my Womb Rabbit is hidden in her Bald Moist Burrow.
 Her knees are by my chest so I use them to help me move my arse back and forth. Another carpet burner I'm afraid.

Bob

Lay The Table

"Pass the salt, dear."…..or should I say
"Put your Fish Fork in my Fish Pie, dear."
Lol

I like to be wined and dined then screwed on the kitchen table.
I lift my legs up high and Bob grabs my arse.
 I love this.
Make sure you use a disposable table cloth, it could get messy.

Brenda

1
2
3
4
5
6
7
8
9
10
11
12
13
14
15
16
17
18
19
20
21
22
23
24
25
26
27
28
29
30
31
32
33
34
35
36
37
38
39
40
41
42
43
44
45
46
47
48
49
50
51
52
53
54
55
56
57
58
59
60
61
62
63
64
65
66
67
68
69
70
71
72
73
74
75
76
77
78
79
80
81
82
83
84
85
86
87
88
89
90
91
92
93
94
95
96

The Magic Scissors

Did you know that 'The Scissors' is a position normally done by lesbians?
Add the word 'Magic' and it becomes our position. Lol

To get into this position takes practice but when Bob has me in this position he puts his Glue Stick in my Fuzzy Felt Hole and starts his thrusting. My arm aches like hell but it's worth the pain to enjoy this magic position.

Brenda

Over The Edge

What I really love about this position is that Brenda might fall off the end of the bed. Lol

I sometimes pretend to lose control of my legs so Brenda falls on her arse.

I lie on the edge of the bed with my legs over the end. Brenda opens her Willy Sleeping Bag and sits on my Mushroom Head.
Be careful Brenda, health and safety comes first. Lol

Bob

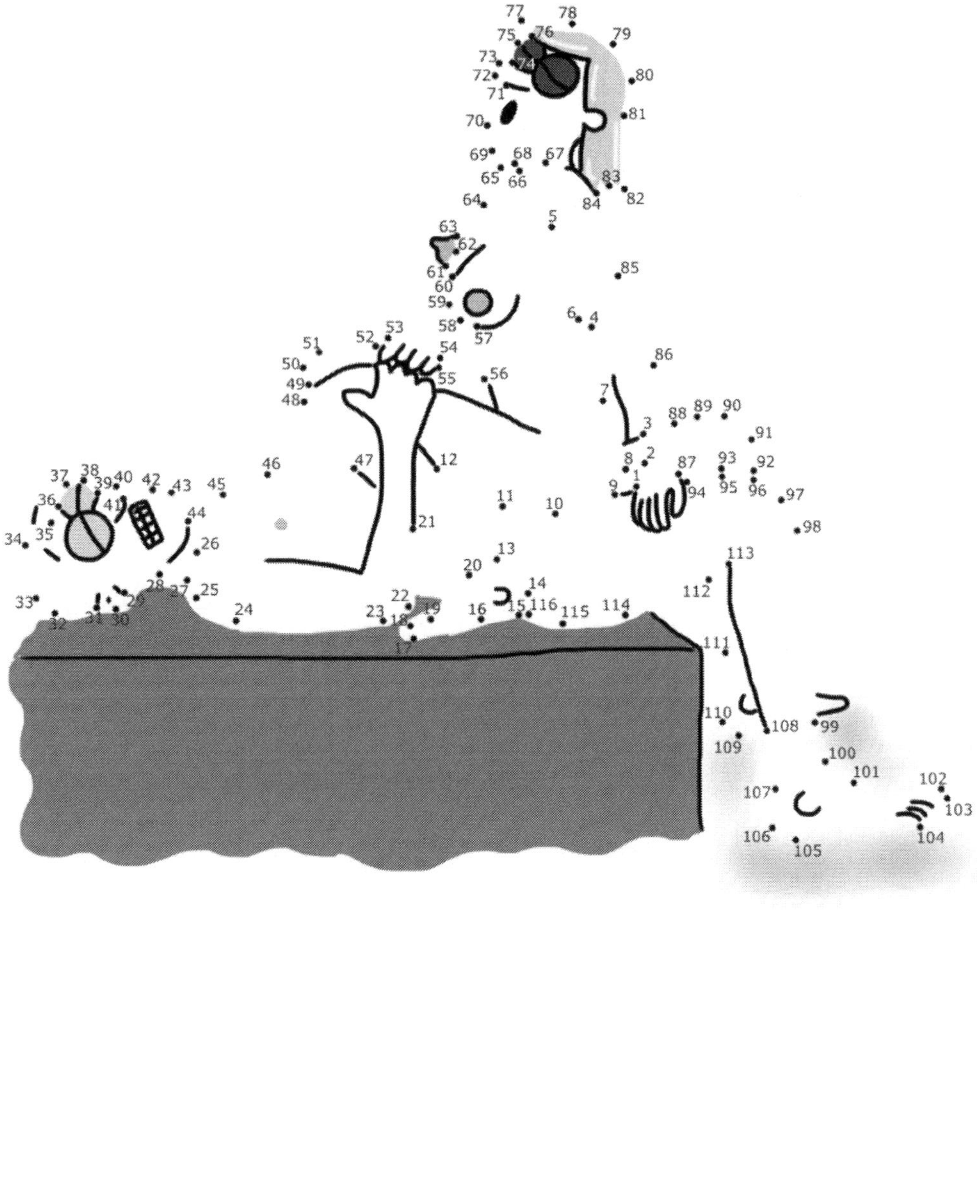

Put Your Feet Up

When I get home from work I like to shower then relax and put my feet up. Unfortunately, if I tell Brenda I want to put my feet up she instantly gets all horny because she thinks I want to do this position.

I lie on the floor with my feet on the bed. Brenda sits on my John Thomas and moves her Lasagne Lips up and down. I love this position, even when Brenda spits in my face for a laugh.
Stupid cow.

Bob

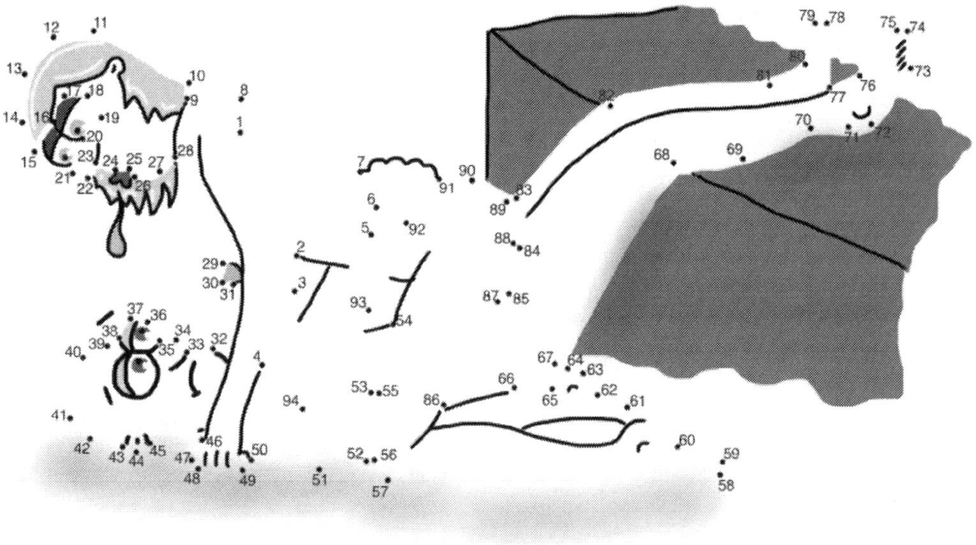

Santa Baby

I know this isn't officially a sex position but it reminds me of when I was a kid.

Every Christmas I would sit on Santa's knee and tell him what I wanted for Christmas.
It wasn't really Santa of course. It was Mr Griffiths from the market. He used to make us reach into his pocket to get a sweetie.

Dirty bastard!!

Brenda

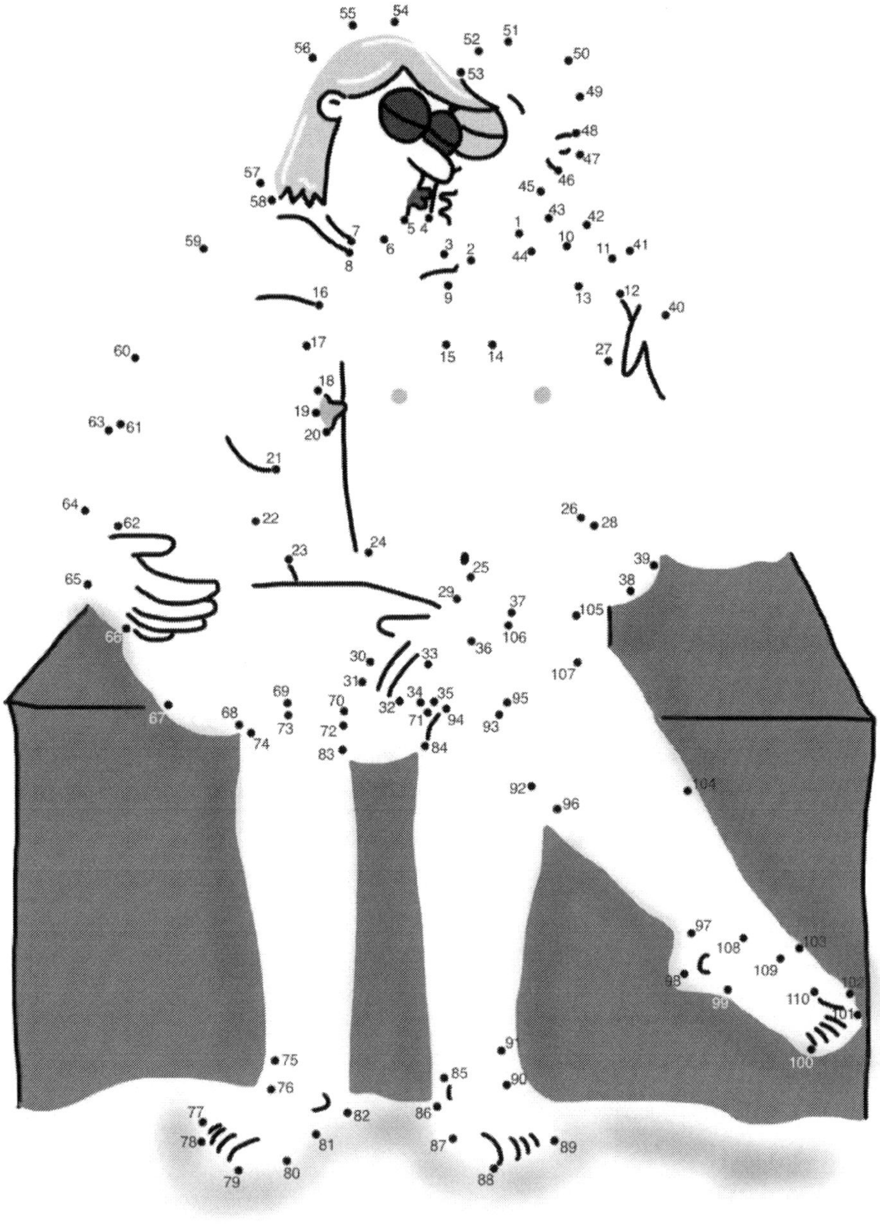

The Sea Lion

Have you ever been to the zoo and watched the animals shagging?
Bob likes to watch the elephants, he says it reminds him of his ex-girlfriend.
Lol

I've never seen a sea lion shag but I'm guessing it looks like this.
I lie on my front with my upper body raised on my elbows. Bob lies on top of me with his Cock in my Slash. Movement is slow and grinding.
It's a nice and relaxing shag.

Arf Arf Arf Arf. I love it.

Brenda

Side Saddler

The posh and rich ladies like to ride side saddle....On horses.
Brenda isn't posh or rich but still likes to ride side saddle....On my Tackle.

Brenda lies on her back with both legs in the air. I pull her legs to one side then enter her Cunny with my Tackle. I then pump and pump until she's saddle sore.

Sorry Brenda. Lol

Bob

The Spine Breaker

The reason this is called 'The spine breaker' is obvious. It nearly breaks your spine to do it.
You have to be very flexible and flexibility is something I have buckets of.

I sit on Bobs face then bend my back until I'm able to suck on his Vomit Pole.
Bob can have a good lick of my Fuzzy Snake Pit too.

Brenda

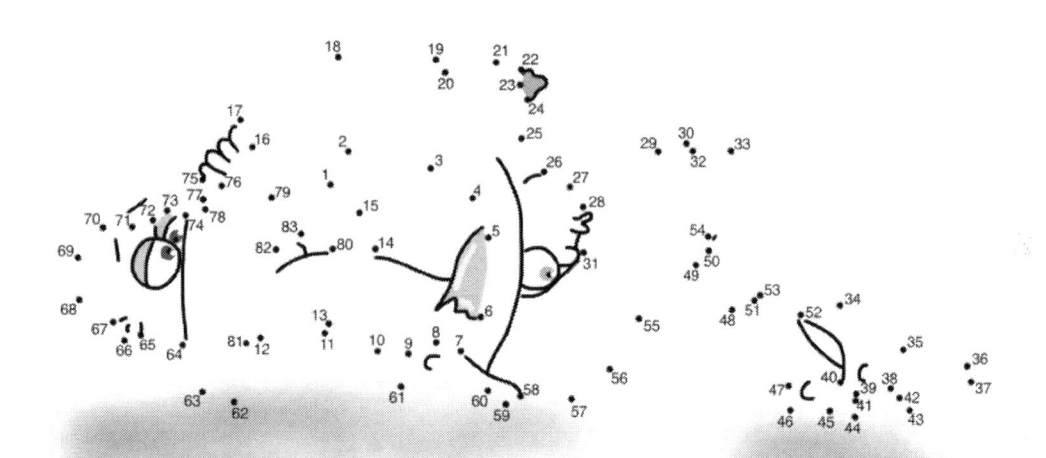

Bob

Name : Bob
Age : 45
Hair Colour : Skin
Eye Colour : Brown
Star sign : Cancer
Occupation : Entertainer
Favourite Book : Bob and Brenda's Joke Books
Favourite Film : Bambi
Favourite TV Program : South park
Favourite Food : Brenda's snatch
Hobbies : Wanking

The Squashed Snake

This position looks like a crime scene to me.
A loving couple murdered in the middle of getting it on. Lol

I'm lying on my back on the floor and Brenda lies on top of me with her back facing me. I put my Trouser Python into her Rabbit Hole and we are good to go. To be honest it's hard to go anywhere in this position.

More carpet burns I suppose.

Bob

The Supermarket Trolley

I hate going to the supermarket.
So when Brenda asked me if I wanted to push the trolley tonight, a feeling of doom came over me.
How was I to know she meant this position.

Brenda bends forward and I enter my Pound into her Slot and grab hold of her wrists and wheeeeee ....
Clean up on aisle two.

Love it.

Bob

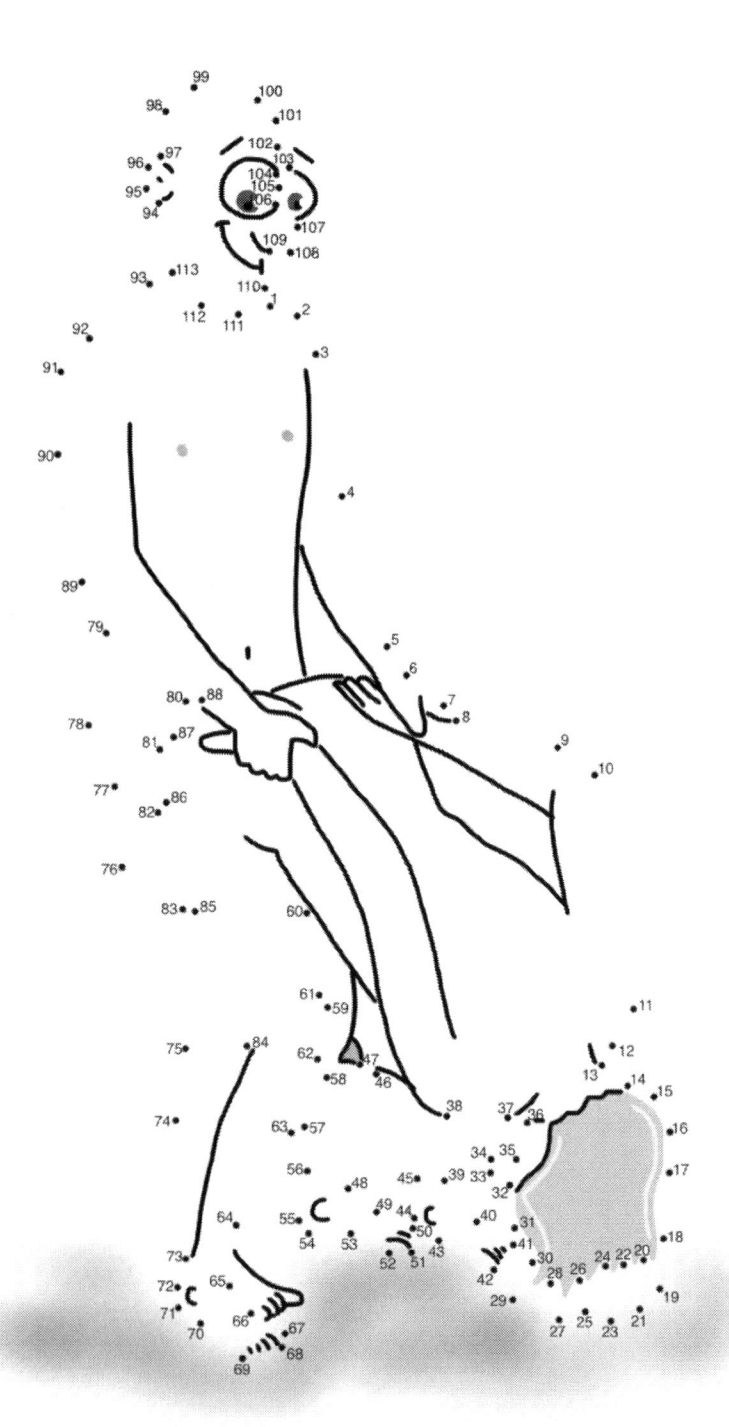

The Super Rimmer

Is it a bird? Is it a plane? No, it's Brenda the Super Rimmer. Lol
This is something you really have to try, just once.

I bend over and use the wall to keep me balanced. Brenda climbs onto my back with her head facing my arse. She then leans forward so she can rim my Brown Button.
I make sure I'm clean before hand and wind free. Lol

Bob

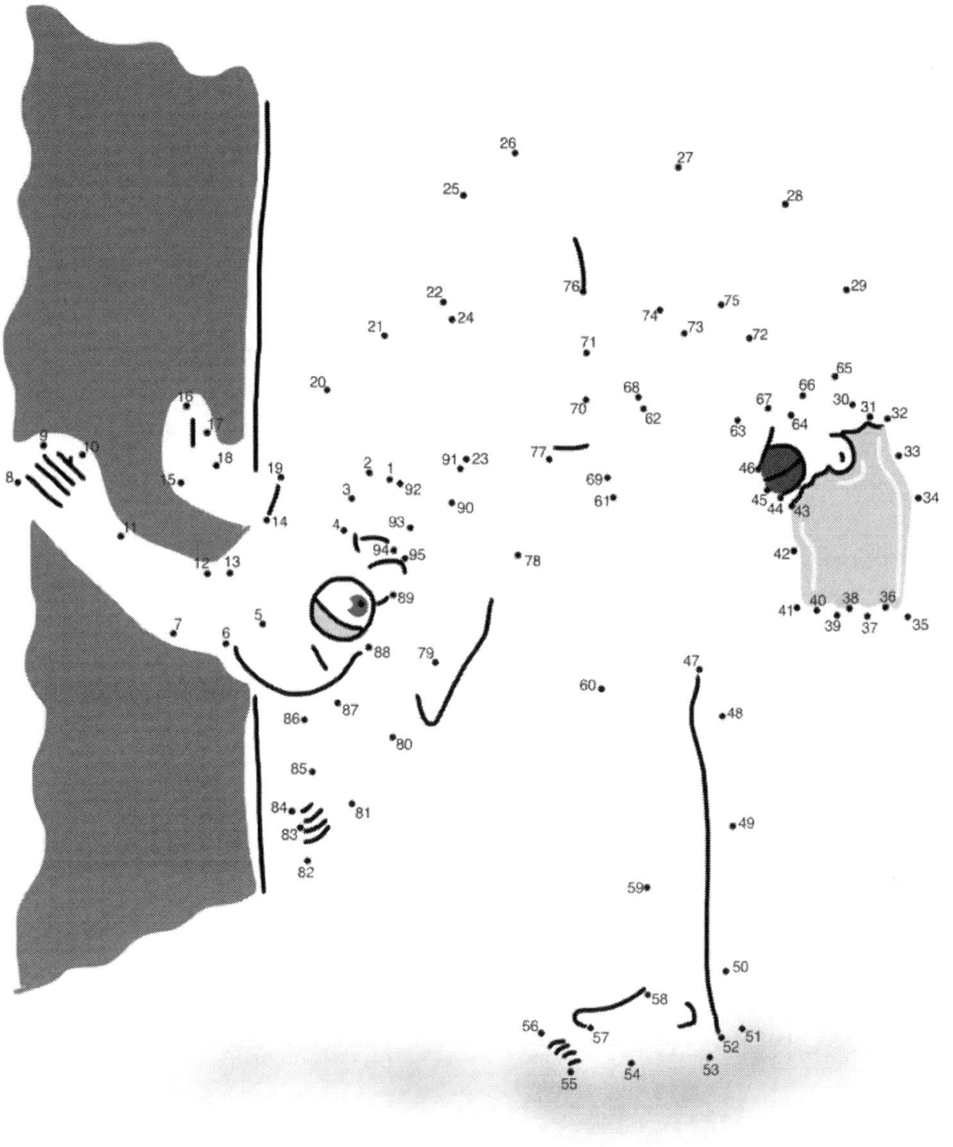

Swivel On This

If you're lucky enough to have a girlfriend who has a slim body like Brenda then doing this position will be a breeze.
If she has the body of an elephant then you're screwed. Lol

I pick Brenda up and she wraps her legs around me. I put my Ding Dong in her Slime Hole. This helps me hold her up while I move her up and down on my Todger.

I also get to give her arse a good grope. Mmmmmmmmm.

Bob

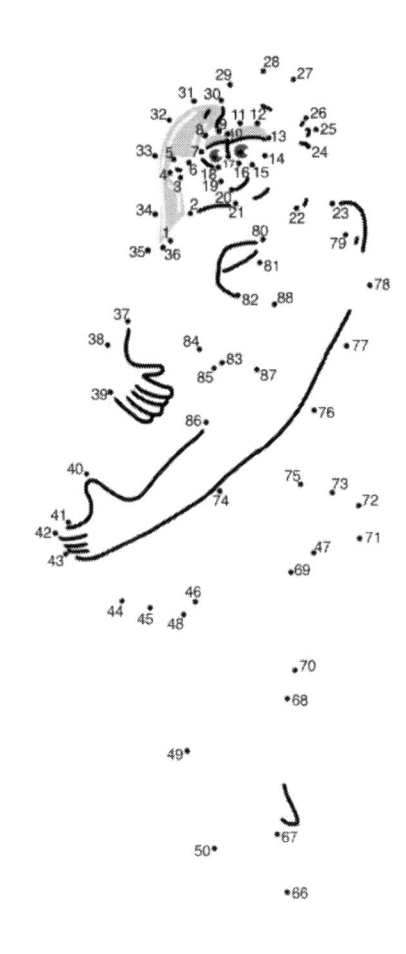

Tickle My Fancy

I love having my fancy tickled. Whether it's Bobs tongue, finger or power tools. I love it.

If I lie on my side Bob can enter my Muff from behind with his Growler and tickle my Muff Nose with his fat fingers.

I love this one.

Brenda

Tippy Toed

The things I do for Brenda.
The 'Tippy toed' is a position that really hurts my toes and we usually end up falling over.

I crouch down and balance on my tippy toes. Brenda sits on my lap then my Sniffler enters her Smelly Slanted Smile and we slowly move until we fall over.

Lol

Bob

Up Periscope

We sometimes play naval games in the bedroom.

I lie on my back with my legs up by my chest. Brenda sits on my Womb Periscope. She rides me until her Velvet-Lined Meat Wallet has been seasick all down my back.

Dive, dive, dive.

Bob

The Wall Banger

I love this position because it gives Bob the chance to be forceful with me.

He pushes me against the wall and tells me to spread my legs. He then searches my Front Butt with his Love Rod.

I don't know what he's expecting to find up there but he can search all night if he wants.
Lol

Brenda

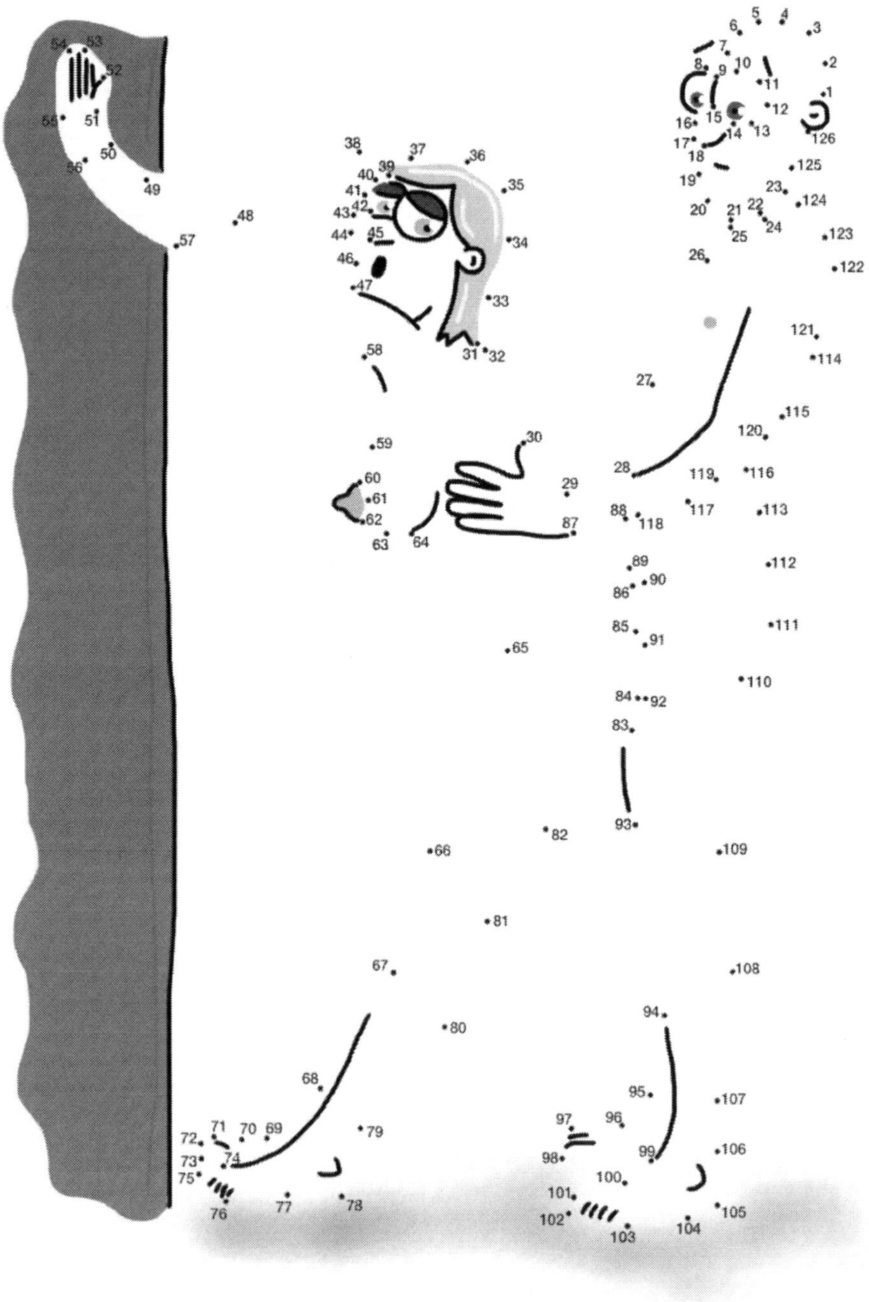

The Wobble Chair

Brenda loves to have a laugh when having sex. This position always has her in fits of laughter.

I lie on my back and pull my legs up to my chest. Brenda then sits on my Dickie. She tries her best to stop her Joy Tunnel from slipping off.

It's a bit wobbly but lots of fun.

Bob

The Wrap Around

There's nothing I like more than a good hug and snog. If Bob's Spam Javelin happens to be in my Stinky Pink Hole then that's even better.

Bob sits on the floor and I straddle him and wrap my legs around his back. This is another carpet burner.

More scabs on my arse. Ouch!!

Brenda

You Rub My Back And I'll Rub Yours

I love a good massage and I love a good rogering. With this position I get both at the same time. It's a win, win situation.

Bob sits on the floor and I reverse myself onto his Meat Popsicle and lay my head on the floor. Bob can then rub my back whilst my Sweaty Love Box gets a pounding.
It's kinda like a lazy mans doggy style.

Brenda

A Word From The Author

I would like to take this opportunity to thank you for buying this book and to thank you for your ongoing support. Without you, Bob and Brenda would still be a day dream in my head.
Since 2012 Bob and Brenda have sold thousands of books all over the world, from the UK to India and Australia.
I hope you continue to support Bob and Brenda because this is just the tip of the iceberg.
Bob and Brenda have some new exciting adventures to come.
Thank you.

Paul Gwilliam

Spot the difference : Answers

Printed in Great Britain
by Amazon